PETER FRASER
HILL OF FEARN

PRIME MINISTER OF NEW ZEALAND
1940 – 49

Marjorie E. Taylor

Published by Fearn Community Council

First printed 2006

Printed and Produced by D-Tech. Telephone 01436 821501

Copyright © 2005 Fearn Community Council

ISBN Nos: 09552381-0-2   978-0-9552381-0-9

Prime Minister of New Zealand
1940 -1949

The Rt. Hon. Peter Fraser P.C. C.H.
Born and Educated at Hill of Fearn, Ross-shire, Scotland
1884 – 1950

FOREWARD

In 2003, when Hill of Fearn School named its newly refurbished library after Peter Fraser, there was a display of photographs and copies of newspaper reports on Mr Fraser's visits to this area, and of other important events in the life of this famous former pupil of the school. The marvellous display had been organised by Mrs Jean Cheyne who with her helpers had researched and arranged the exhibits. It is from the work done at that time that the idea of this book was born.

Peter Fraser left Fearn to work in London and emigrated to New Zealand where he continued his activities in the unions and the Labour Party. In 1918 he entered parliament as one of a very small group of Labour MPs. Just over twenty years later he was to reach the country's highest office as Prime Minister, holding this post throughout the momentous years of World War ll and becoming a much respected world statesman.

As a small boy, I met Peter Fraser when he called on my parents and two aunts during his visit over New Year 1949. My father said that, although he left Scotland as a young man, Peter Fraser always maintained a close interest in his home area. On his visits, though time was always limited, he loved meeting old friends. He also took a keen interest in the opportunities that were available to the school children and the young people of the area.

I remember the excitement in the school when a plaque in his memory was unveiled in 1956 and also the visit of the New Zealand High Commissioner in 1984 to commemorate the 100th anniversary of his birth. I am therefore delighted that this book has been published as it gives us a lasting record of his life and all that he achieved.

George Ross
Rhynie House
Hill of Fearn   May 2005

ACKNOWLEDGEMENTS

It has given me considerable pleasure, with the assistance of Jean Cheyne, to record the life of the Rt Hon Peter Fraser P.C. C.H. Born and educated at Hill of Fearn in the late 1800s and rising to world eminence, his career is most worthy of note. With the passage of time, little is now known about him locally. So it seems most appropriate, as we approach 100 years since Peter's departure from Ross-shire in 1906, that we put on lasting record an insight into the life of this distinguished gentleman of whom Fearn can feel justifiably proud.

I am indebted to my friend, Jean Cheyne, who has freely shared with me the archive material of her private collection from several years of research. Ruth MacLeod's enthusiasm in the early stages laid the foundation for this publication which has been commissioned by Fearn Community Council. She has also supported Jean with research, and assistance through the print process. Thanks must go to Mark Ferguson and his team at D-Tech for his excellent guidance and patience throughout the book layout, development and printing.

Hill of Fearn Primary School and many local people from their family collections have provided relevant material or photographs, and Jean has made every effort to locate photographic ownership for permission to use in this book. As there are a few exceptions, we shall be pleased to acknowledge these in later reprints.

We are grateful for the major contributions from George and Isabel Ross of Rhynie House; Mr & Mrs Alexander Mackenzie of Fraser Cottage; Mrs Ann Fraser, Inverness; Mrs Donetta Matheson, Tain. Thanks must go to Donald and Karen Ross for making time during their holiday in New Zealand to do a little research and to David Watt of the Ross-shire Journal, for access to the Peter Fraser collection of news clips and documents put together by his grandfather at The Ross-shire offices. These have been supplemented by reports from The North Star, The People's Journal, Daily Record, Aberdeen Press and Journal, Derbyshire Evening News, The Times, The Scotsman, The Standard of New Zealand; and copyright permission for the Gordon Minhinnick sketch from The New Zealand Herald. Thanks is extended also to cartographer Wendy Price for the attractive map design, and copyright in this publication.

Permission for the reprint of postcards has been gratefully received from Mr Dudley Gordon of Fearn, Tain Museum and The Reference Library at Farraline Park, Inverness.

Permission for use of photographs has been kindly granted by: The Imperial War Museum, London; ITN Archives - British Pathe; The Alexander Turnbull Library and National Archives, Wellington, New Zealand and The John Curtin Prime Ministerial Library, Perth, Australia.

For those who would wish to know more about the life of Peter Fraser, the excellent book, *'To-morrow Comes the Song'* by joint authors Michael Bassett and Michael King of New Zealand comes highly recommended. Both authors have visited Hill of Fearn. Other background information is available from *'Peter Fraser: New Zealand's Wartime Prime Minister'* by James Thorn, and *'Peter Fraser – Master Politician'* edited by Margaret Clark. An historical record on the life of Peter Fraser is kept at the Tarbat Discovery Centre at Portmahomack, Ross-shire

Author's Note

Before embarking on this project, I had limited knowledge of Peter Fraser. As the book evolved, I learned so much and my respect and admiration for him grew.

I hope that, through the pages of this little book, you too will grow to appreciate the very special qualities of a remarkable man.

Marjorie E. Taylor   October 2005

CHAPTER I

1884 – 1910

Today, a neat cottage close to the village school in Hill of Fearn bears a modest plaque telling passers-by that it is the birthplace of Peter Fraser. At the time of his birth, no-one in the small Ross-shire village imagined that – from the humblest of beginnings – wee Peter was destined to become an international statesman and Prime Minister of New Zealand during the Second World War.

Peter Fraser's ancestors were caught up in the Highland Clearances, which began towards the end of the eighteenth century. It was a time of major change throughout the land. In parts of Sutherland and Ross-shire, some cottagers and tenant farmers were systematically driven from their homes. It is recorded that large numbers emigrated to South Africa, North America, Australia and New Zealand. We are told that some did find work in the new woolgrowing industry. Others had to find employment fishing along the coast of the Dornoch and Moray Firths, while a few skilled tradesmen such as carpenters or shoemakers stayed in Highland villages. Traditions that had been centuries in the making were shattered. Shocking stories of indignities and brutality lived on in local memory and these had a profound influence on young Peter.

Peter's mother's family were directly affected by the Clearances in Sutherland. Stories were passed down of the burning of his grandfather's home near Rogart and of banishment from the land farmed by the family for generations. His grandfather, Peter MacLeod, moved south and in the 1830's set up as a carpenter in Fearn. There he married Margaret Holmes and Peter's mother, Isabella, was born in 1849.

Peter's father, Donald Fraser, was born in 1845. Donald lived at Balmuchy near Hill of Fearn where his father, Alexander, worked as a blacksmith. The family ancestors were of the Clan Fraser of Lovat from the west shores of Loch Ness. Although caught up in the Highland Clearances, they were not evicted. However, with the dispersal of the clan structure after Culloden and the coming of the sheep, they were no longer able to sustain a living at the family trade as blacksmiths. An iron smelter in the vicinity of Fearn attracted the Frasers to Easter Ross in the late 1700s.

Donald and Isabella met as children. A close friendship had already developed before Donald quit working as a shoemaker and emigrated to Canada in 1872 in search of a better life. Tiring of frontier life with the NW Mounted Police, he left Manitoba and travelled east. Isabella joined him in Montreal and they married there in 1875. Soon after, they returned to Hill of Fearn, where they acquired a small three-roomed cottage onto which, with his Canadian savings, Donald built a workshop. From there he established a shoemaker's business. Within the humble cottage they raised their large family. Their seventh child, Peter, was born at Fearn on 28 August 1884.

Fraser Cottage, Hill of Fearn 1941

Peter was one of eight children born to Donald and Isabella:

Alexander	born 1 May	1876	-	apprentice to his father
Johan Margaret		1877	-	emigrated to South Africa
William		1879	-	moved to London
John		1880	-	died in infancy
Christina		1881	-	emigrated to South Africa
Mary		1882	-	died in infancy
Peter	**28 August**	**1884**	-	**emigrated to New Zealand**
Donald		1886	-	emigrated to Canada

Poverty, disease and infant mortality were rife in Victorian times; and like many other Highland families, the Fraser household was affected by the frequent presence of sickness and death. It is thought that an attack of measles in early childhood was responsible for Peter's impaired vision. Nevertheless, when he joined his sisters and his brother, William, at the village school in 1889 he was quickly recognised as a gifted pupil. Fortunately, elementary education in Scotland became free that same year (two years ahead of England and Wales). It was a comprehensive education and Peter clearly loved study. His progress was a source of pride and watched with keen interest by many in the parish including one of his teachers, Miss Bain.

School Street, Fearn

School Street in the village of Fearn in the late1800's

Peter made lasting friendships at Fearn school and was affectionately known throughout his life as 'Pat' by friends and family. However, he did find the school building stark and cold, despite efforts to warm the rooms with open fires, and likened it to a prison. In later years, as Minister of Education in New Zealand, he emphasised the importance of comfort and pleasant surroundings for school children. The headmaster of the time, Donald MacArthur, was a dominie of the old type. Typical of his profession he turned out with fortitude and patience many able men in science and medicine. A firm believer in the value of teaching the three Rs and a strict disciplinarian, Donald MacArthur ruled the school with a rod of iron. It would never have occurred to him that he was nurturing a future Prime Minister of one of the most loyal of all British Dominions.

Peter was fortunate that both his parents could contribute to his education, teaching him not only the history of the MacLeod and Fraser clans but also Scottish history, especially relating to the Highland Clearances. They fired Peter's lifelong interest in the meaning of words, his sense of injustice and the wish to put things right.

Despite poor eyesight, Peter seems to have keenly enjoyed physical education too. His involvement in long-jumping, curling and hammer-throwing is recorded and it is known that he particularly enjoyed long walks in the countryside. Though unable to participate fully in ball games, his capacity for organisation was developing and he became secretary of the local football club.

Peter's early life was influenced by the church and the current political climate. The Fraser family attended the Fearn Free Church just outside the village. The division in the Church of Scotland of 1843 had brought about this strict new religion: regular attendance was compulsory and there was a rigid code of everyday conduct. Peter built up a very broad knowledge of scripture from long, obligatory church attendance and seemingly endless sermons. Every evening at the family home a chapter of the Bible would be read aloud.

Secondary education was not free in 1898 when family pressures made it necessary for young Peter to quit full-time schooling. At the age of 14, he took temporary employment (delivering newspapers and telegrams and as a relief postman) until he was old enough to take up an apprenticeship as a carpenter. His deliveries entailed walking in all weathers between Fearn and Portmahomack. Peter felt there was an injustice in the non-provision of suitable warm clothing: his mother had to pack newspaper inside his jacket for warmth and insulation. If ever he had power, he would do something to correct such a matter. He began to think not only of benefits for postboys but how many other desirable ends might be attained. Peter would rest for an hour or two at the Carnegie Library in Portmahomack, making very good use of the reading facilities available to him there, before his long walk back to Fearn. By the time he was offered a permanent position as postman, he had saved sufficient to buy himself a bicycle. At the same time, and on the advice of the headmaster, his parents agreed that Peter should attend night school two evenings a week. In due course he obtained his Merit Certificate which was the highest qualification available to him. Even at this early age he clearly believed in discipline. He applied it to himself and was to demand it from colleagues and associates throughout his life.

Peter's parents were a handsome and very striking couple, both speaking Gaelic. They were deeply religious, highly respected and very popular within Fearn and the surrounding community. In the difficult economic climate of the time,

Fearn Post Office

Fearn Post Office c. late 1800's from where Peter embarked upon his working life as a postboy

Donald 'one of nature's gentlemen' struggled to make a living as a shoemaker, whilst Isabella ran the spartan home: seeing to the family needs, fetching water from the well and spinning wool to supplement the family income. Isabella was a gentle, refined lady, highly intelligent, very well-read and a supporter of the Women's Suffragette Movement.

The Fraser home was a political household where, we are told, meals and the discussion of local and national issues went together. Donald's workshop was known locally as 'The House of Commons', where the men of the village gathered regularly to discuss and debate political issues. Peter and his school friends (one being Kenneth MacLeod of Elm Cottage), although not allowed to participate, would attend the 'Parliamentary' discussions. The young lads revelled in the stormy debates among the older men. The meetings were greatly enhanced by the arrival of the arch-conservative headmaster, Donald MacArthur, who would add fire and brimstone to the debates. It was here in his father's workshop that Peter received his political education and at this early age he was already formulating ideas for the betterment of mankind. All were welcome at 'The House of Commons' and there were no political hostilities outwith 'The Chamber'. Mr John Campbell, a schoolmaster and later headmaster at Fearn School, remarked in the Aberdeen Press and Journal that the men of the village showed 'a very high standard of self-cultivated intelligence'. As the leading member of the Scottish Liberal Party in the district, Donald Fraser campaigned tirelessly for electoral reform. There was much rejoicing when he and fellow members of 'The House of

Peter Fraser

A recruit of the Seaforth Highlanders Volunteer Corps
c. 1902

Commons' were enfranchised for the first time to vote at the general election in December 1885. Growing up in this period of ideological political ferment, Peter became secretary of the Fearn Young Liberals League and, over time, developed the art of heckling those with whom he disagreed.

In 1901, at the age of 16, Peter began his five-year apprenticeship with Alexander Mackenzie, a local carpenter in Fearn. The workshops were based at Caberfeidh. He was paid the princely sum of 5 shillings a week (25 pence). He later transferred as an improver to James Nicol, a builder in Tain. It is believed that his poor eyesight was a significant drawback. He continued to pursue self-improvement and developed a life-long love of drama, poetry and literature. He was a bright, pleasant and impressionable lad with rapidly developing verbal skills. He was a leading light in the formation of a local debating society held in Fearn School, bringing together young men of his own age to argue and debate over the major topics of the day. He joined the Tain Literary Society and the Tain Independent Order of Good Templars (a Masonic temperance movement) and he spent several years with the Seaforth Highlanders (known locally as 'The Ross-shire Buffs').

The Good Templars supported political equality for women and measures that would combat the health and social problems caused by excessive use of alcohol. Peter involved himself in the Order for five years. During this period he learned much about committee procedure and held every office within the Order – rising to Lodge Deputy, the highest position. Records show that, by the time he was 20, wrestling with political issues gave him the greatest enjoyment. His social conscience was strong and he could be moved to genuine indignation over the plight of people disadvantaged because of poverty or class. It was through the Good Templars that he first met members of the new Independent Labour Party including Keir Hardie, an early leader. It is recorded that Peter was being drawn to the left yet he retained affection for the Scottish Liberals and the friends he had made within their midst. His horizons were widening.

Peter continued to live with his parents while still indentured and soon there was scarcely a cause in the district with which he was not involved. He did not have enough time for courting and even less for the football club. He helped to recruit members for the Rural Labourers' League and strongly supported the Scottish Small Landholders Movement (retaining his link with that group even after he left Scotland). We are told that by now Peter was the complete political enthusiast: the world needed correcting and he was going to have a part in the process.

He wanted to see something of the wider world and learn more about politics. So he left Hill of Fearn in 1906, when he had completed his apprenticeship. Employment was scarce. Initially he was briefly employed as a journeyman carpenter in Edinburgh, then he worked for a while as a dock labourer in Leith. He left in support of four fellow-employees who were sacked – unfairly in Peter's estimation. Several casual jobs in Glasgow followed before he travelled south to London, where his brother, William, was active in the printing chapel at the Amalgamated Press. Peter bought his first spectacles and soon found employment as a carpenter on the White City site at Shepherds Bush. Thanks to the influence of his father's friend, James Galloway Weir, Liberal MP for Ross and Cromarty, Peter was later hired by the Board of Works, which was in charge of several major projects – including improvements within the House of Commons. Peter worked there till 1910.

There is scant information about Peter Fraser's life in London. It is likely that he would continue to attend self-improvement classes and he was certainly able to indulge his interest in the theatre. It is known that he listened to soap-box orators and participated in public speaking in Hyde Park. He supported women's suffrage, assisting at meetings organised by Emmeline Pankhurst. Through his brother, William, he also joined the Clarion Fellowship, which promoted socialist activities. However, his fascination with politics clearly received its greatest stimulation at the House of Commons and no doubt he listened to as many debates as possible.

While Peter's personal life in London is only briefly recorded, historical records show that he had arrived at a most propitious time. Exciting developments in Westminster began with the resignation of the Liberal Prime Minister, Sir Henry Campbell-Bannerman. Within days Herbert Henry Asquith took his place, and his new Cabinet included young Winston Churchill and David Lloyd George. But the progress of 'New Liberalism' seemed slow and Peter was losing confidence in the Liberals. It is recorded that by this time he and his brother were attending meetings of the Independent Labour Party. Soon he would tear himself away from old political loyalties as left-wing ideas inspired him more and more.

It was during his employment in Westminster that Peter first heard about New Zealand, a country already largely free of the class system he deplored. In London he would meet people who knew about the country's liberal reforms. Sir Joseph Ward, the Liberal Prime Minister of New Zealand, was in London in 1909 to attend the Imperial Naval Conference, and he was warmly received by Asquith at the House of Commons. Sir Joseph never let a moment pass without promoting his country. At this time, Peter Fraser could not have imagined that within a decade he and Sir Joseph Ward would be parliamentary colleagues on the other side of the world. Among other influential and enthusiastic ambassadors promoting the political advancement of New Zealand was Tom Mann – a British radical, leader of the Labour Party at Westminster for over 50 years – whom Peter met in 1910.

He was certainly aware of New Zealand's reputation as an enlightened country; but it was a sudden change in his job prospects that precipitated Peter's decision to move on. Towards the end of 1910 the work programme at the House of Commons was trimmed back and one of the two carpenters in the section was to be made redundant. Being unmarried, Peter stood aside and, unable to find alternative work, he set sail for Auckland in November that same year. He was 26 years old.

CHAPTER 2

1911 - 1935

On arrival in New Zealand in early January 1911, Peter Fraser found accommodation in a respectable boarding house and worked for a while as a casual labourer on the Auckland waterfront handling cargo, as he had done in earlier years in Leith. Later he took a job as a general labourer, drainlaying or working on roads and footpaths. He soon found Auckland Public Library housing the best collection of books in the country. He frequented the Library regularly – even at week-ends and on public holidays. There he formed close links with Tom Bloodworth, a fellow carpenter, and through him was introduced to the Auckland Socialist Party. The ASP provided him with a social network and brought him into contact with folk who would be his comrades for life.

Supporting the
General Labourer's
strike in Auckland
October 1911

Personally familiar with the effects of inequality, want and poverty, Peter was intrigued to find that there was growing discontent among workers in a land that seemed so socially advanced. The ferment at grass roots was a heady challenge for him and, in due course, he was to participate in events that led to protests and strikes – and be identified as the cause of some of them! Eighteen months on, he had learned a great deal about his new country and about the trustworthiness of the workers' opponents. He had witnessed the limits to worker solidarity and he knew who were his true friends, whose loyalty he could rely on. He quickly became one of the ASP's most effective soap-box orators. Those who listened realised he was devoid of malice and had a strong sense of fairness. In the future his ability and honesty would be recognised by all.

Peter's unwavering efforts on behalf of miners and manual workers on the North Island not only occupied every waking moment but also were to land him in trouble with the law. At a rally in October 1913, Peter was one of those addressing the crowd. Soon police officers arrived in force and he was among the large numbers arrested. He was released after three weeks, only when sureties for £600 had been arranged. In 1916 he was to find himself behind bars again, serving a twelve-month sentence for openly opposing conscription. Becoming increasingly critical of the atrocities of the Great War, Peter and other Labour leaders who opposed conscription were systematically arrested and put behind bars by the coalition government, thus removing the best Labour brains from the political scene and beleaguering the Labour Party.

In later years Peter was questioned about opposition to New Zealand's participation in the Great War and his subsequent support for the country's involvement in World War ll. For Peter there was no incongruity. He believed that the First World War had been a conflict between imperial powers – its only relevance for workers being that they had provided the cannon fodder. Men were to die whilst others became rich. World War ll had been started by right-wing reactionary forces out to crush the legitimate political expression of workers' rights with the ruthless destruction of working-class movements.

While in prison, Peter read whatever he could lay his hands on – books on economics, the Russian revolutions, Karl Marx, and possibly also Parliament's Standing Orders and Speakers' Rulings. He emerged in December of 1917 with a considerable grasp of parliamentary procedure and had become a less revolutionary and more practical politician.

The establishment and growth of the new Social Democratic Party had taken Peter away from Auckland. He worked unpaid for the SDP and took casual work on the waterfront in Wellington to pay for his board and lodgings. He then found a role as a journalist and for a short spell acted as Editor of the Maoriland Worker (to which he continued to make contributions throughout the 1920s).

In 1918 he was elected president of the Wellington SDP, which became the stepping stone to his nomination as a Labour candidate in the Wellington Central by-election of that year.

On 3 October 1918, Peter received a rousing reception when he rose to address the crowd on the announcement of his success at the polls. He had won by a large majority over three other candidates. As the Labour Member of Parliament representing the Wellington Central Constituency at the age of 34, Peter Fraser was now the newest and youngest Member of Parliament where the average age was 51 years. The occasion was tinged with sadness for Peter. Although his mother would learn of his success, his father, to whom he owed so much, had died five weeks before word could reach him.

Peter Fraser – MP 1918

Some years earlier, Peter had met George and Janet Kemp at an ASP supper. We are told that George was fond of liquor and had a roving eye. By early 1917 he had left Janet and his young son, Harold, for good. He found employment as a clerk in Wellington, formed a relationship with another woman and eventually remarried.

Janet Kemp was also a native of Scotland, born and educated in Glasgow where she taught orphaned or abandoned children. She emigrated to New Zealand with her family in 1909. Janet was a vigourous and witty speaker who liked addressing meetings. Regarded as a force among the Labour Party faithful, she was a founding member of the Women's Progressive Society. As a voluntary health worker, Janet was appointed to fill a vacancy on the Wellington Health Board. She spent ten years on the Board, topping the polls in 1933. She was considered to be an intellectual and, although she was renowned for her kindness to those in need, she could certainly fight for her beliefs. It is known that Peter had always keenly supported better opportunities for women and he seems to have communicated with Janet on these issues through the pages of the Maoriland Worker. At what point his relationship with Janet became serious is unclear but their friendship blossomed after George Kemp's departure.

In the puritanical environment of the time, they maintained separate establishments until they married in Wellington in 1919. Peter was attracted to Janet by her intelligence, her gentle voice and her interest in socialist literature. She was a dignified, gracious lady, tall and slim with dark eyes, a most able woman who added to her husband's influence in the Labour movement. Janet was always a perfect hostess. Their loving relationship lasted till her death in 1945. Throughout those 26 years, she shared Peter's political passions, looked after him to the best of her ability (he was seldom at home) and involved herself in a variety of women's causes – always with his approval and support. Together they regularly attended WEA lectures and summer schools with Tim Armstrong and other friends.

Janet Fraser - 1925

Peter enjoyed the company of children and particularly of his young stepson. Speculation about his remaining childless may well be explained by the fact that Peter's family had been affected by psychiatric illness in an age when mental health problems were considered a stain on any family's good name. Even today, such problems are likely to be talked about in whispers. Peter's concern about his family's psychiatric history almost certainly contributed to his lifelong interest in mental illness.

Peter's journey to Parliament had been anything but smooth. However, along the way he showed canny common sense and had become a skilled negotiator, an accomplished conciliator and someone who saw further ahead than most people. These skills would prove invaluable. In the years that followed, the relationship between the Labour and opposition parties grew more strained. The emergence of the NZ Communist Party was also a bugbear. Peter fought hard to ensure Communism was distanced from the Labour Party. In fact, seventeen very difficult years were to pass before the Labour Party came to power – a far longer uphill climb than any of the activists had expected.

It took the Great Depression, major unemployment and years of conflict and endurance before an extra 150,000 votes gave Labour its long-sought victory. We are told that those longing for certainty in uncertain times developed a profound respect for Peter Fraser and a readiness to follow him wherever he led. They elected a disciplined force with a coherent programme of state interventions. After political campaigning for 25 years at a level of intensity that would have worn down lesser men, the Labour Party was on the threshold of achieving things. It was 1935 and Peter was 51 years old.

The two years before the Labour Party swept to victory had been a period of both sunshine and shadow in Peter's personal life. He and Janet were delighted when her son Harold married Hairini, daughter of Tim Armstrong, Peter's long-time friend and colleague. That joy was a double delight when baby Alice was born in March 1934. Peter and Janet adored Alice.

Janet and Peter Fraser - 1933

Sadly, Janet's health became a cause for concern that same year. She had contracted tuberculosis, and the worry affected Peter's own health for a while. As she slowly recovered Peter wisely decided that they both needed a proper holiday. In early 1935 they sailed for London. The long journey provided them with much interest as the ship took them westward via Tasmania and Australia, Colombo, Bombay and the Suez Canal. It was the first time Peter and Janet had left New Zealand since their separate arrival a quarter of a century before. Their main purpose was to return to Scotland together.

In the long months stretching before them they were able to visit the Irish Free State. and the time spent in London gave them special pleasure. Useful contacts were made, and Peter took the opportunity to attend the Empire Parliamentary Association Conference and the British Trade Union Congress. Eventually their planned itinerary came to an end and they were free to travel north. Stopping first in Glasgow, they spent time with Janet's family and friends. They also looked over a new housing development for single women. Then they met up with Peter's old friend Tom Skinner, living by this time in Inverness. Peter and Tom corresponded throughout their lives since sharing so many interests as young apprentices in Fearn – Peter as a carpenter and Tom as a baker. Soon Peter and Janet made their way to Hill of Fearn, where Peter showed Janet his birthplace and his school and introduced her to friends still in the neighbourhood. Sadly, his parents and eldest brother, Alexander, had died several years earlier. Their graves stand close to the main door of Fearn Abbey. His surviving brothers and sisters had left the village years before.

Walks and drives beside the Moray Firth, frequently in the company of Tom Skinner, were enjoyed well into September. Janet was restored to good health and enchanted with the Highlands. The long period of uninterrupted time together was coming to an end. All too soon they crossed the Atlantic and, after a brief time in New York, travelled by train to Toronto to visit Peter's youngest brother, Donald; thence to Vancouver where contact was made with several Fraser and MacLeod relatives. A ship from the west coast took them to New Zealand and they were back in Wellington by the end of October. The momentous 1935 general election was but a month away.

On every count, the six-month trip had been a success. Peter met people and confronted issues that would be important to him, and to New Zealand, during the next 15 years of his life. Janet was well again and ready to support him in the gruelling ministerial career about to begin. With her help and encouragement he was becoming Labour's best all-round politician. They would return to Scotland in 1944, but the trip would be accompanied by the stress of office and a recurrence of Janet's respiratory problems.

CHAPTER 3

❀

1935 – 1939

The first Labour Cabinet of New Zealand - 1935
Front Row: Parry : Peter Fraser : Michael Savage : Walter Nash : Fagan : Semple

We are told that something akin to an electoral earth-quake occurred on 27th November 1935, when the Labour Party won the general election with more than 47 per cent of the total vote. After so long a journey to power, its senior members now faced the biggest challenge of their lives.

New Zealand's first Labour Cabinet was formed without delay and Peter Fraser took on a huge work-load. Besides being Deputy Prime Minister, he became Minister of Education, Minister of Health, Minister in Charge of Mental Hospitals, Inspection of Machinery and the Marine and Police Departments. Now in a position to pursue his vision of securing true equality of opportunity for all New Zealanders, Peter would implement much of the new government's social policy. It is recorded that few, if any, of the politicians of his day matched his energy and his single-minded concentration on building the first really prosperous nation in the South Seas. With Janet's steadfast support, he regularly worked a gruelling 17-hour day.

Peter Fraser
Deputy Prime Minister of
New Zealand

He had been the party spokesman on Education since the early 1920s. New Labour legislation would now attract more candidates to the teaching profession, reinstate admission to school at age 5, reduce class sizes and, in due course, would provide free education for every youngster until age 19. Kindergartens, universities, school dental clinics, the provision of free school milk and special measures for facilitating remote and rural education would all benefit from Peter's intervention. In retrospect, these developments may be seen as the prototype for New Zealand's present-day concept of seamless educational development throughout life.

Shortly after Peter had become MP for Wellington Central in 1918, a seat he was to hold for the rest of his life, the influenza pandemic reached the country's North Island. It is hard to credit that, throughout the world, the disease claimed more lives than the number who perished in the Great War, which had just ended. Certainly, it claimed over five thousand victims in New Zealand and tens of thousands suffered including, at length, Peter Fraser himself. In the efforts to control the disease, he gave a devoted and tireless service which was never forgotten. Heedless of the risks he faced, his dedication did much to seal his position in his Wellington constituency. Thereafter, whatever may have been thought about his politics, Peter's humanity was never questioned. Afterwards he assisted in the development of his party's Health policy for over a decade and his appointment as Minister of Health in the new Labour Cabinet was a logical progression.

Peter's thinking about health care had moved him in the direction of greater state involvement. The experiences of the epidemic lay behind Labour's increasing interest in a nation-wide health system. Now Peter was able to set the wheels in motion. Innovations would include the establishment of a Medical Research Council to correlate the medical research being undertaken throughout the country; and the introduction of diphtheria inoculations – eventually measles and whooping cough vaccinations too – as standard features in all primary schools. New legislation would increase the number of health care staff at every level. Pay and working conditions across the board would be improved, and health services would become increasingly centralised.

The health, education and economic position of Maori had been of particular concern to Peter for a number of years. He could relate to the thorny issue of land alienation and its impact on the people's welfare, seeing in the Maori displacement from their land a parallel with crofters in the Highland Clearances. While land policy had been central to all governments' relationships with Maori since the time of European settlement, the new Labour government was more sensitive to the problem than its predecessors. Peter was now in a position to take decisive action. School medical officers and district nurses were appointed to ensure regular visits to remote Maori schools, and action was taken to improve nutrition and drinking water supplies. These remedies were to have a positive effect on death rates and infant mortality. Equal entitlement to welfare benefits and improvements to the rules governing old age benefit would follow.

It is recorded that Peter had a delicate mission at first as the new Minister of Police. He had, after all, spent 12 months in jail soon after settling in New Zealand. However, the wary relationship between him and the Commissioner had warmed to one of mutual respect within a year. The Commissioner realised that Peter was intent on gaining more money for the police and that he was a man whose word could be trusted. Peter's recognition of the New Zealand Police Association was greatly appreciated. This had a positive effect on staff morale and efficiency. Reduced hours, higher pay and improved working conditions would make recruiting easy; and Peter would eventually be instrumental in opening the police force to female recruits. In the years that followed, he and the Commissioner would enjoy a close working relationship.

His Marine portfolio provided Peter with contacts that would be useful to him for the rest of his life, and his friendship with F. P. Walsh of the Seamen's Union developed into a close working alliance. Peter had worked on the waterfront and a significant number of the country's seamen were enrolled in his Wellington Central electorate. Now he could ensure that legislation was introduced to govern maritime safety, shipping, fisheries inspections and marine research.

The first three years of Labour government brought a rapid decline in unemployment. Numerous projects were launched for the building of schools, hospitals and state housing, power and drainage schemes, new transport and telephone links and the establishment of a Country Library Service. Memories of the Great Depression had faded. The impact of reforms and improvements was being felt nation-wide and there was an air of optimism everywhere. It was not surprising that Prime Minister Michael Savage and his Labour colleagues were returned for a second term in the 1938 general election. Nor was it surprising that New Zealand was living beyond its means.

Immediate steps were taken to stabilise the economy without lowering living standards. The government continued to spend but attempted rigidly to control prices and wages. All imports and exports were licensed and, with support from unions and manufacturers, efforts to stimulate domestic manufacturing were increased.

At the same time, the Prime Minister's health, which had been the subject of speculation and conjecture for several months, became a real worry. He had an abdominal operation in August 1939 but it was clear that the prognosis was not promising. From that time onwards, Peter Fraser virtually assumed the Prime Minister's responsibilities.

Janet and Peter Fraser at Christmas
Because of her work with Maori, Janet was known as 'Te Whaea o te Katoa'
'The Mother of us All'

CHAPTER 4

1939 – 1940

The deteriorating international situation reached a crisis point in late August 1939. Rebels in the Labour Party chose this moment to become more unruly and disruptive. One dissident in particular (bitter for a long time because he was not in the Cabinet, and holding the ailing Prime Minister responsible for that exclusion) became more unpleasant and malicious than hitherto – thereby revealing his unsuitability for high office and eventually effecting his own expulsion from the Labour Party. The rebels' antics consumed a considerable amount of Peter's energy as the Prime Minister's health caused increasing concern; but foreign affairs had to be top of the Cabinet's agenda for, on 1st September 1939, Hitler invaded Poland and Britain declared itself at war with Germany.

Having already signified its support for the mother country in such an eventuality, New Zealand slipped into war mode smoothly and efficiently. Thanks to Peter Fraser and his officials, a Council of Defence was already operational and plans for the civil and military aspects of any developing hostilities were already established. It is recorded that all necessary legislation was in place to safeguard ports and vital points against sabotage. A system of reporting ships and aircraft was devised. Suspected dangerous aliens were rounded up and interned. Committees and various groups to study individual problems or carry out special tasks were already at work.

Swift action was imperative. A large number of strict regulations came into force immediately to guard against war-time speculation and the hoarding of goods and to prohibit activities deemed injurious to the common good. Prime Minister Michael Savage and his colleagues were determined that the situation that had arisen in the Great War – enabling some folk to get rich while others were dying in combat on the other side of the world – would not be repeated. To this end many more controls and regulations would follow as the Second World War progressed.

The Prime Minister being unfit to travel, it fell to Peter Fraser to attend the meeting of ministers from the Dominions in London in early October. First there was an Australian Cabinet meeting, and Janet accompanied Peter to Sydney then returned to Wellington. Meanwhile, Peter continued his journey north by flying boat, train and ship to England – a ten-day trip and probably Peter's first flight.

For several exhausting weeks, meeting followed meeting. Peter took advantage of opportunities to make it plain that the New Zealand government wanted a clear statement of war aims – hoping to ensure that if a peaceful solution could yet be engineered, positive steps would be taken. He promised that New Zealand (regarding itself as a country particularly suited to the production of foodstuffs) would do all it could to feed Britain. He announced that some 12,000 New Zealanders had already volunteered for military service and were in training. He made it clear that his country was willing to send troops to Europe, though this would depend on an assessment of Japanese intentions in the Pacific. The fact that Japan was currently preoccupied with China convinced Peter that an attack on New Zealand was improbable and arrangements for mobilization commenced.

Peter requested an adequate British naval escort for his country's First Echelon. Securing such an escort brought him face to face for the first time with Winston Churchill, newly appointed First Lord of the Admiralty. We are told that a cordial and business-like relationship developed between them during the next six years. Churchill praised New Zealand's defence strategy, reporting to the British War Cabinet he thought that country's recognition of the war situation was particularly realistic.

Peter was the first to admit that he had little knowledge of military matters so, while still in London, he sought a General Officer Commanding (GOC) for the New Zealand forces coming to Europe. His country wanted a New Zealand division whose commander had complete control of it and was answerable to the New Zealand government – a force proud of its own identity, not an integral part of the British army. Acting on recommendations from top brass and being a clever judge of character, Peter engaged Major General Bernard Freyberg on his government's behalf. The appointment raised praise from all quarters. In later years it was observed that the personal links forged among Winston Churchill, Peter Fraser and Bernard Freyberg were of untold importance to wartime New Zealand.

These things having been accomplished, Peter was free to accept an invitation to speak to the Empire Parliamentary Association at the House of Commons. His speech was well received. Clearly, New Zealand's Deputy Prime Minister was earning further commendation as a straight talker and a thoughtful advocate, from a country engaged in social reforms that British Labour MPs hoped to emulate. He was able to renew acquaintance with Clement Attlee and with Tom Mann, whom he had first met in 1910.

Later he made contact with brother William, after years of intermittent communication. Eventually he slipped away to meet his childhood friend, Tom Skinner, and spent a few days in his beloved Scottish Highlands. Peter took the opportunity to revisit Hill of Fearn. There, he and William received a warm welcome from their elderly aunts, Betsy and Georgina MacLeod, living on Fraser Street. Peter paid tribute to the modern education in the Highlands on his visit to Fearn School on 28th November. As Minister of Education for New Zealand he could see that great progress had been made since his childhood. He felt that the children received greater opportunities than in the past. Vivid memories of lengthy, uninteresting talks by visitors to Fearn School in his own young days made Peter want to stimulate the pupils. He ensured his talk to the senior classes was as interesting as possible, explaining all that he had seen on his long journey from New Zealand. He did not think that they were bored. Finally, Peter attended a dinner in Glasgow as a guest of honour at the city's Chamber of Commerce then returned to London for a final round of important meetings.

Hill of Fearn School
The stark building which greatly influenced Peter Fraser as Minister of Education in New Zealand to ensure comfort and pleasant surroundings for school children.

On his visits to Fearn, Peter called at the workshops where he served his apprenticeship as
a carpenter with Alexander Mackenzie

| Alex More | Donald MacCorquidale | John Macdonald | Alexander Mackenzie |
| (Blacksmith) | (Carpenter) | (Carpenter) | (Master Carpenter, Undertaker) |

The carpenter's workshops, timber sheds and wood yards were situated immediately beyond the
low dark garage – stretching inwards from the road.

When the provision of equipment for the Royal NZ Air Force, the shipping of the First Echelon to the Middle East and matters relating to war funding had all been dealt with satisfactorily, it was time to head for home.

On the long homeward journey, Peter was struck down with severe food poisoning in Karachi. Though he never touched alcohol by choice, his travelling companions persuaded him to take a tot of medicinal brandy. It worked. Nearer home the journey broke briefly for discussions with Australian government and military chiefs in Melbourne. On Christmas Day 1939, Peter and his companions arrived in Wellington to a very warm welcome. There is no doubt that Peter's warmest welcome came from Janet and little Alice, who were waiting for him on the quayside.

The First Echelon sailed for the Middle East on 5th January 1940 with a battleship escort. The welfare and safety of the troops were of paramount importance not only to the Deputy Prime Minister but also to the newly-appointed GOC. Before embarking with them, Bernard Freyberg had been given considerable discretion over spending on behalf of his men and had hammered out the terms of his own charter with government ministers. Peter Fraser was deeply enmeshed in the affairs of state and working intolerably long hours. It must have been a great relief to him to know that at least one major responsibility was in the capable hands of a man who was to become a lifelong friend and trusted confidant.

That farewell ceremony at Wellington harbour on 5th January was to be Prime Minister Michael Savage's last public function. Those gathered for the annual Labour Party conference two months later learned of the gravity of his illness. It is recorded that he died within hours of hearing that delegates had expelled his most hostile and scurrilous critic. A much loved and respected man, Michael Savage was buried on 31st March 1940 with a crowd of more than 200,000 lining the route to his final resting place in Auckland.

Peter Fraser and General Bernard Freyberg arrive in New Zealand. 1939

Hill of Fearn
From the Gaelic word *Fearna* meaning *Alder Tree*

A'Mhanachainn Rois – Place of the Monastery or Abbey of Ross-shire

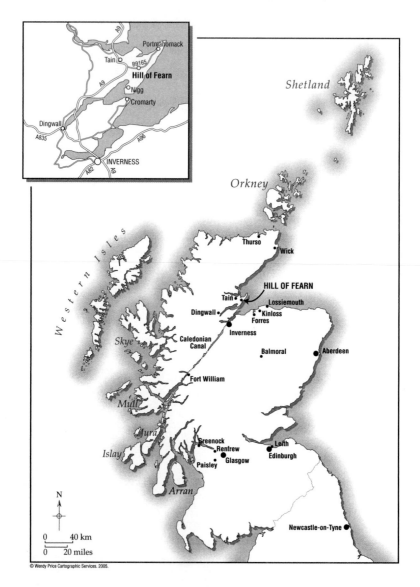

Locations visited by Peter Fraser on his tour of Scotland 1941

CHAPTER 5

1940 – 1942

The Governor-General of New Zealand invited Peter Fraser to form a government and he readily accepted the challenge in early April 1940, receiving a unanimous vote of confidence from Labour Party supporters. He was 55 years old when he became New Zealand's Prime Minister.

We are told that no New Zealand leader before or since has had so much power in his hands as Peter received in 1940. The way he used that power ultimately became the measure of his greatness. With his well-balanced knowledge of constitutional history and the skill to weigh the propriety of actions before taking them, he was to win the widest respect in his adopted country.

Politics that had seemed to consume his life now did so almost entirely. Totally preoccupied with domestic and foreign matters, he had even less time now to indulge in his lifelong love of books and the theatre – and no time at all to lecture publicly, as once he had done, on topics such as the life and work of William Morris or the poetry of Robert Burns. Such were the pressures that he moved with considerable reluctance to the Prime Minister's suite in Parliament Buildings, leaving messengers to shift his books and papers. The task of moving from his cosy home to the official residence, overlooking the harbour and closer to the office, was left almost entirely to Janet.

In that first year of Peter's premiership, the war in Europe escalated, spreading with frightening speed. By April 1940 a total of nearly 35,000 had volunteered to join New Zealand's armed forces; New Zealand's First Echelon was safely encamped at El Maadi just outside Cairo; and the Second Echelon, including a Maori Battalion, was preparing to embark for rigorous training sessions in the United Kingdom. In spite of the burden of so many other responsibilities, Peter took a close personal interest in convoy arrangements and ports of call. When told there was difficulty disembarking the Maori Battalion in South Africa, because of concern about its reception on racial grounds, he authorised the commanding officer to arrange a bus to take the troops round Cape Town for a day. He also backed Freyberg's judgement about where the Second Echelon should be stationed in Britain.

Meanwhile Bernard Freyberg was spending much of his time deflecting efforts by British HQ in Egypt to break up his troops into separate detachments for general use throughout the Middle East – clearly in contravention of his understanding that New Zealanders would be deployed as a single entity. Despite strenuous efforts, disaster did occur.

The potential for mix-up was always there: communications were frequently delayed and battle plans were, of necessity, cryptic. Believing that General Wavell's command had New Zealand government sanction, Freyberg allowed his men to join two Australian divisions and a British armoured brigade in defence of Greece. Bernard Freyberg and his troops were already committed before Peter found out. Currently in Egypt to visit as many New Zealand soldiers as possible, to assure them of his interest in their welfare, Peter had foreseen the true state of affairs more shrewdly than General Wavell and the British Cabinet. He correctly guessed that the Greeks might well collapse before a German onslaught. They did.

The long and sorry saga caused military humiliation for the Allies. The Greek army's capitulation left a small force lacking support from air fighters and heavy bombers and woefully short of ammunition supplies. Hopelessly outnumbered and under severe air attack, retreating men were stranded on Crete. The military blunder resulted in heavy casualties; and to his horror, Peter learned that General Wavell had cabled Bernard Freyberg in his name, requesting him to surrender since no more ships were available to complete the evacuation. Always at his

Speaking with New Zealand military engineers at El Maadi, near Cairo. May 1941

best in a crisis, Peter sprang into action, and as a result of his intervention nearly 4,000 extra stranded troops were evacuated from the Greek island, including 700 New Zealanders. His presence in the Middle East at that time could not have been more fortuitous.

With New Zeland nurses at Cairo, during his visit to the Middle East.

In later years the disaster of Greece and Crete weighed heavily on Peter's mind. The battle had cost New Zealand dearly, despite his own efforts at the time of the evacuation. Inwardly he blamed himself; and it is recorded that his anxiety to see that such a situation was not repeated was almost certainly a factor in his postwar interest in national service.

As the Nazi machine rolled across Europe and threatened to cross the English Channel, threats closer to home caused alarm. The realisation that several shipping lanes within New Zealand's territorial waters had been mined evoked a clear feeling among the wider public that the country needed to raise its level of commitment to winning the war. Part of the Third Echelon was despatched to Fiji to form a garrison there. Recruiting enough men for the war effort became the principal challenge, but volunteer numbers had tapered off. There was no option but to contemplate conscription.

The subject was, of course, fraught with political difficulties because it conflicted with the traditional attitude of the Labour Party. Peter grasped the nettle. First, he consulted his colleague F.P. Walsh about possible reaction within the union movement: soundings revealed that a majority would support conscription if it went beyond men and included land and property. It was a time of deep concern, but full trust was placed in the Prime Minister and his Cabinet to use their powers wisely. Peter now possessed the necessary authority to pursue the war diligently.

A War Cabinet was established, consisting of two Labour ministers and two opposition representatives and chaired by the Prime Minister. Peter's respect for opposition member, Gordon Coates, grew quickly. Here was a man who worked hard and whose word could be relied on – a man who was genuine, warm and understanding. A relationship as close and trusting as it was unlikely developed between them.

Gordon Coates was commissioned to review all aspects of New Zealand's defence readiness. The War Cabinet was prepared for action if hostility was shown by Japan. The review concluded that provision for this to succeed was woefully inadequate: much ammunition and weaponry had been sent to Britain to assist with invasion preparation there, and New Zealand did not have enough equipment or trained troops to stave off even a small attack.

It was decided that the country would have to look to North America for military hardware; and conscription became a reality after July 1940, when voluntary enlistment ceased and men were chosen by ballot. Steps were taken to conscript wealth – by requiring thousands of individuals and companies to contribute towards war loans; by directing farmers about what they could do with their land; by identifying relevant overseas assets that could be realised for war purposes; and by assuming the power to requisition factories and plant.

No one could have foreseen just how long the Second World War would last – or how many demands would have to be met in defence of democracy. Country after country became heavily involved. Peter Fraser had always been single-minded about his causes, and the defeat of Hitler was now paramount. He was determined that people everywhere should put the war first in their thinking.

There was something about all those years of planning for a Labour victory in the House of Representatives that had given Peter considerable skills as a strategist; and he grew in stature during the war as his mind grappled with innumerable daily problems, many requiring immediate decisions. Narrow prejudices of the 1930's were gone, and he was thinking about global issues as never before. He felt strongly that maintaining the right psychological approach to war was important, and that it would be disastrous if a mood of defeatism was allowed to develop anywhere within the Commonwealth. It must have been difficult at times to keep optimism alive, for setbacks and disasters were numerous and the world faced dark days.

The New Zealand government had to maintain the closest possible contact with its Allies, in spite of the fact that overseas travel had become extremely hazardous. Leaving his deputy Walter Nash as Acting Prime Minister, Peter travelled to London in June 1941. The original plan for a gathering of

Commonwealth leaders came to nothing; but Peter was warmly welcomed at No.10 Downing Street (his first meeting with the British War Cabinet) then joined Prime Minister Winston Churchill as a guest at Chequers. The absence of other Commonwealth leaders maximised Peter's access to Churchill and he attended more than a dozen meetings of the War Cabinet between June and August. He also had several meetings with Labour party members, Clement Attlee and Hugh Dalton.

He interspersed his attendance at Whitehall with a round of official functions. On 25th June he dined at Buckingham Palace and next day was sworn as a Privy Councillor. He attended an American Independence Day luncheon on 4th July, and was again given a rousing reception by the Empire Parliamentary Association gathered at the House of Commons. He visited docks, toured bomb sites to meet survivors and rescue teams and, whenever opportunity presented itself, he met New Zealand servicemen stationed throughout the United Kingdom to assist in various war-related activities.

Visiting Wales, he received the Freedom of the City of Cardiff. Travelling northward, he visited Coventry and Birmingham, Liverpool and Manchester, and came at length to his beloved Scotland. He combined official duties with private visits; and during his northern tour he received an Honorary Degree at the University of Aberdeen and the Freedom of that City and of Glasgow and of Inverness. Revisiting Leith and Edinburgh and making a brief courtesy call at Balmoral, Peter was in Inverness for the important Freedom ceremony on 1st August 1941.

Peter was able to take several days off to spend time with his friend Tom Skinner and to bask in the warmth of the Highland welcome awaiting him in Ross-shire. The welcome in Hill of Fearn was the warmest of all. Flags borrowed from the Harbour Master at Portmahomack flew from the housetops, hedgerows and garden fences. The gathering that had been planned for the village hall had to be transferred to the school playground: more than 1,000 friends and well-wishers from all parts of Easter Ross assembled to meet him on 4th August. Among them were boyhood friends, and he was presented with a silver-mounted morocco case to hold the illuminated address sent to him the previous year, when he became Prime Minister. Peter's happiness would have been complete if Janet had been at his side; but brother William was there to join in the festivities and accompanied him on a visit to their childhood home, now named Fraser Cottage and occupied by local postman Mr Duncan Gray and his wife. This occasion was the climax to a day when Peter had received the Freedom of the Royal Burgh of Tain. At Tain Parish Church, after a very moving ceremony, the presentation of the burgess ticket and casket was made by a member of his own clan, Provost William Fraser.

HOME-COMING OF
The Right Hon. Peter Fraser

PRIME MINISTER OF NEW ZEALAND.

A PUBLIC MEETING
—Will be held in—
The HALL, HILL OF FEARN
On Monday, 4th August, 1941

at 8 p.m.

To Welcome Fearn's Distinguished Son.

HECTOR MUNRO, Esq., late of Fearn, will preside.

It is hoped all old and new friends, neighbours and well-wishers will be present, as it is the known wish of Mr Fraser to meet as many as possible in a friendly, homely and informal atmosphere.

Community Singing - - David Mackenzie, Esq., Conductor.

A Silver Mounted Morocco Roll Case will be presented to Mr Fraser from his many friends, old and new, in Fearn and surrounding districts.

The Fearn Home Guard will furnish a Guard of Honour, together with A.R.P. Services. Inspection of Home Guard at 7.30 p.m. approximately in Playground of Public School, thereafter March Past at War Memorial, where the Prime Minister of New Zealand will take the Salute and lay a Wreath.

Buses from and to Inver, Portmahomack, Hilton, Balintore and Tain are being arranged for.

The Committee extend a cordial invitation to all.

GOD SAVE THE KING.

Printed by James L. Shand, The St. Duthus Press, King Street, Tain

Peter Fraser laid a wreath at the base of the War memorial at Fearn
There followed a salute to the Home Guard on parade. 1941

At Fearn School, accompanied by Mrs Murray, Commandant, and Capt Geo Gordon
Mr Fraser inspects Fearn ARP.   He is seen speaking to Mrs Douglas. 1941

Peter Fraser leaving the home of his aunt, on Fraser Street, Fearn. August. 1941
L to R Thomas Skinner : William Fraser : Peter Fraser : Kenneth M MacLeod

Using Fearn as a base, Peter travelled to Wick and Thurso to meet New Zealand personnel at Coastal Command and operational stations. He visited Fearn school and had an informal talk with pupils and staff. The school presented him with a small gift and to mark the occasion the remainder of the day was observed as a school holiday. On 6th August, he received the Freedom of Dingwall, county town of his native Ross-shire – the fifth burgess ticket he had acquired since coming to Scotland. On the Dingwall burgess roll, his signature was added to a list that included such famous names as William Ewart Gladstone, Lord Roseberry, Joseph Chamberlain, Lloyd George and Andrew Carnegie. All too soon, world affairs were again clamouring for attention and, at the end of a memorable and happy week, he departed for the south after calling on New Zealand RAF servicemen stationed along the Moray coast at Forres, Kinloss and Lossiemouth. He travelled via the Caledonian Canal to the west coast where he addressed a large gathering of people at the Fort William Hotel.

Back in London, Peter studied and enthusiastically endorsed the Atlantic Charter (outlining British and American post-war aims) just drafted by Winston Churchill and President Roosevelt. When a second attempt failed to organise the meeting of Commonwealth leaders, Peter was free to depart from Whitehall, and we are told he felt it essential to return home via North America to obtain an up-to-date assessment of Pacific affairs. The journey westward took him and his companions via Dublin and Newfoundland.

'Good-bye : God Bless You : God Bless New Zealand'
Winston Churchill bids farewell to Peter Fraser on his departure for New Zealand
21 August 1941

There are few recorded details of his meeting with the American President or his meeting with Canadian ministers in Ottawa several days later. We do know there was much sharing of information and Peter was greatly encouraged by the talks. While still in Canada, he visited New Zealand airmen in training in Ontario, Manitoba and Saskatchewan. He arrived home on 13th September to find that, although Walter Nash had held things together, the government had lost popularity during his long absence.

The Japanese bombing of Pearl Harbor and invasion of the Philippines in December 1941 took the Allies by surprise, and over Christmas and New Year a real sense of emergency gripped New Zealanders for the first time since the war had begun. The pressures on Peter Fraser were immense: domestic politicking was rife, and the best of the country's young men were thousands of miles away helping in the European conflict.

It is not surprising that, as he coped with endless daily stress, Peter's health would begin to give Janet cause for concern. Fatigue would attack the iron constitution that had kept him going for so long. He was usually at his desk until well after midnight; he did not eat properly, unless Janet was at hand, and skipped meals or survived on a diet of toast or tea and cream cakes; he took no exercise and rarely relaxed. Worse still, his limited eyesight was deteriorating. Her concern was not misplaced. Nevertheless, he continued to combine his duties as Prime Minister with long-held responsibilities relating to the Audit Office, the Legislative Department, etc, and as Minister of Police and acting Minister of Finance.

The prospect of another official trip to North America in August 1942 seemed to be a long-awaited opportunity for Janet to accompany Peter and combine business with pleasure. Her dedication to her wartime duties as one of the country's foremost social workers was making its demands on her own constitution. She felt they both needed a holiday and she longed for time alone with him – to read, to talk, and just be together. Sadly, her trip was cancelled because of the fighting in the Pacific, and Peter travelled without her.

He stayed as the President's guest in the White House. A strong bond was formed as they exchanged information and confidences. He also met State Department officials and military leaders, the British and Russian Ambassadors, and President Roosevelt's close confidant, Harry Hopkins, whom he liked particularly. On his 58th birthday, Peter received a note from Mark Twain's son telling him he had been elected an honorary member of the International Mark Twain Society. The honour had probably been instigated by the White House, and Peter was delighted.

Before leaving Washington, Peter spent a useful few days with his Deputy, Walter Nash, who was on a two-year assignment at the New Zealand legation. Flying to Canada, he saw his brother Donald briefly in Toronto, then moved east to Ottawa for lengthy discussions with Prime Minister Mackenzie King and his ministers. Risky and uncomfortable as it was, air travel did enable leaders in World War ll to share confidences and exchange information to an unprecedented extent and so reduce the need for more-formal conferences.

Peter flew home to deal with growing demands from MPs wanting a greater say in the daily decision-making and to grapple with the thorny problems relating to the deployment of New Zealand troops, who were needed in both Europe and the Pacific. Australia's decision to recall her troops completely from the Middle East did nothing to resolve the dilemma.

Throughout his life Peter consumed vast quantities of tea

Peter Fraser, wearing a borrowed beret, takes a moment to relax in the Valtumo area, Italy May 1944

CHAPTER 6

1943 – 1945

The New Year dawned. The war raged on and Japanese tyranny continued to spread its tentacles across the Pacific. In Europe and the Mediterranean there were German defeats and Allied advances. History books show that chaos reigned everywhere. Blood was shed in the Russian battles of Kursk and Leningrad and in fierce combat in Libya and Tunisia, Sicily and Italy.

While New Zealand troops were heavily involved in the fighting on Italian soil, Peter Fraser had to prepare for a fight at home. He was unwell. Debilitating infections plagued him frequently, and almost constant septicaemia and blood-circulation problems threatened to interrupt his punishing work schedule. Sadly, antibiotics were not widely available in those days and prescribed sulpha drugs were sometimes ineffective. Nevertheless, while there was no real enthusiasm for it, a general election in New Zealand became a necessity. There were loud public complaints about wartime regulations and controls, and shortages and rationing elicited bitter dissatisfaction: holding on to power in such a difficult climate required considerable skill. In October 1943 the election took place, Labour returning for a third term, but some of Peter's seasoned colleagues lost their seats.

A few days later, Peter became seriously ill. Pyelitis and resultant complications kept him away from his office for more than two months. It is recorded that in those days his illness would have been life-threatening.

At that time, the Australian government was particularly apprehensive that discussions about the future of the Pacific were already taking place without either Australia or New Zealand being consulted. Indeed, visitors to both countries (including a group of American senators) had voiced the possibility that the United States might seek to locate permanent military bases in the South Pacific. It was thought prudent that the two neighbours should consider the establishment of a framework for closer ties and explore common attitudes to relevant regional issues. Accordingly, just as soon as Peter was well and in command again, he attended a re-scheduled meeting in Canberra.

The five-day conference in the Australian capital resulted in an agreement – the 'Canberra Pact' – in January 1944. This initiated the desired closer collaboration between Australia and New Zealand who, having supported Europe so readily in the theatre of war, felt strongly that they should be consulted on the disposal of enemy territories when peace came to the Pacific. It sought also to establish the foundation for linking economic and social development, such as internationalisation of airlines, after the war.

Peter was averse to future plans for regional security and keen to ensure that any defence zoning would form part of a world-wide system. He particularly hoped that a revived League of Nations, or similar body, would preserve future peace on a global basis. He returned home feeling that the conference had been worth while; and Janet, who had joined other wives attending the gathering, had been able to enjoy her first overseas trip with her husband since 1935. The opportunity for further overseas travel together occurred just two months later.

A Conference of Commonwealth Prime Ministers, meeting as a group for the first time during the war, was to take place in London towards the end of April. Janet accompanied Peter and the ministerial team. They travelled first to the United States. Colleagues were anxious still about Peter's recent health scare. He had no problems: it was Janet who gave cause for concern on the flight, when she experienced breathing difficulties in the unpressurised aircraft and required oxygen.

The party stopped briefly in Washington and lunched with Eleanor Roosevelt at the White House. Peter had an opportunity to attend several important meetings and to address the US Senate about the Australian-New Zealand Agreement, reassuring the senators that there was nothing anti-American in the Canberra Pact – though nothing could disguise the fact that neither country was anticipating allowing military bases on its territory once the war was over. Peter paused for a day at the Conference of International Labour Organisation in Philadelphia, and on arrival in New York he addressed an ANZAC Day ceremony at the Rockefeller Centre. The New Zealanders reached London on 27th April and were to experience directly the food shortages and the effects of German air attacks.

Commonwealth Prime Ministers were briefed about plans for the imminent Allied landings in Normandy. The general direction of the war was widely discussed in a series of meetings with the British War Cabinet, and reports show that Peter exercised considerable influence at the conference. He took the opportunity also to remind the British that they should never take for granted the agreement of his own government when they engaged in military planning. Opportunities for 'freedom of the city' functions and to receive honorary degrees provided light relief for the visiting statesmen. Amidst scenes of splendour on 10th May, Peter received the Freedom of London in the presence of British and

Allied war lords and statesmen in exile. He accepted the honorary Freedom of Derby, but as his many duties made it impossible for him to visit the town, he made arrangements for the New Zealand High Commissioner, Mr W.J. Jordan to attend as his deputy. (The following year in April 1945 he enjoyed a flying visit to Derby to sign the roll of Honorary Freemen of the Borough.) He received the Freedom of the City of Edinburgh on 12th May and attended a degree ceremony at the University of Cambridge seven days later. There he was made an honorary Doctor of Laws. Peter and Janet were also among those invited to Buckingham Palace and met the young Princess Elizabeth for the first time.

H.M. the King entertains Dominion Premiers to dinner at Buckingham Palace 1944

Janet had her own itinerary. She had not recovered fully from her air trip and took things quietly in London. Peter left her there and flew to Italy to visit New Zealand troops and to talk with his GOC, Bernard Freyberg. In his eagerness to keep New Zealanders in Italy, Winston Churchill put his own plane at Peter's disposal.

He flew into the recently liberated Caserta airport near Naples and motored to Monte Cassino. He spent several days with the soldiers at Atina and talked to as many men as he could, outlining rehabilitation plans and listening to their concerns. His genuine interest and relaxed manner made a deep impression on them and added much to his stature as Prime Minister. Moving north, Peter spent time with the Maori Battalion, which had suffered heavy casualties in the recent battle at Cassino. He was clearly impressed by the troops and their officers and keenly interested in the details of a prolonged and costly battle. It is recorded that he also met members of the Polish army who had been involved in the final assault on the monastery; and he was pleasantly surprised to hear the they knew of the New Zealand plan to provide refugee status for several hundred Polish youngsters.

Peter's respect and admiration for his GOC had grown steadily; and it is believed that, while alone with Bernard Freyberg, Peter sounded him out about the possibility of his becoming New Zealand's new Governor-General at the end of the war. They travelled together to Rome, had talks with Field Marshal Alexander, met several priests who had been assisting New Zealand prisoners of war, and had an audience with Pope Pius XII in the Vatican. Peter was aware that the meeting with the Pope would be welcome news to Roman Catholic friends and supporters at home. In the week that followed, there was an opportunity to fly to Cairo to visit the New Zealand base camp at El Maadi and talk to the troops. On 12th June Peter was back in London to attend a meeting of the British War Cabinet and hear about progress in the Normandy landings.

Peter Fraser on his visit to the Monte Cassino area, Italy. May 1944

Accompanied by General Freyberg   *Addressing New Zealand troops*

Peter and Janet were reunited and travelled north to Scotland to visit New Zealand RAF personnel stationed at Wick and to enjoy a short break in Ross-shire. They received a wonderful welcome from the New Zealand servicemen based at the Royal Naval Air Station at Fearn under the Command of Captain Robertson RN. Sadly, brother William had died during the previous year; but they visited MacLeod relatives living in Tain and enjoyed the company of good friends. They also visited Fraser Cottage, where Mrs Dinah Gray acted as hostess. Peter and Janet stayed next door with Peter's elderly aunt Georgina, while his staff stayed at Fearn Hotel.

On the evening of 19th June, Peter presided at a concert organised by the SWRI, held in Fearn Village Hall to raise funds for 'Salute the Soldier Week'. In true Highland tradition he and his party were piped into the packed hall. After a delightful programme of music and dancing by local talent, Peter spoke of the Normandy landings to the assembled audience. He expressed the view that, although severe fighting still lay ahead, he was confident that the foundations of victory had been laid. Next morning on their brief visit to the school, Janet congratulated the children on their bright appearance and complimented the girls on their splendid exhibition of Scottish country dancing, which she and Peter had so enjoyed the previous evening.

Peter Fraser with Captain Robertson, R.N.
Commanding Officer of the Royal Naval Air Station at Fearn

All too soon, official duties called them back to London and Peter attended another meeting at Downing Street for an update on the military situation. Winston Churchill was full of praise for New Zealand's support and commitment and for Peter's single mindedness throughout the war. Later he was to observe that New Zealand was a most reliable ally and never put a foot wrong.

*The Rt. Hon. Peter Fraser, Prime Minister of New Zealand visits the
Royal Naval Air Station at Fearn 1944*

L. to R. Back Row: Lt. Wilson and two school friends – lady unknown : Kenneth M MacLeod

*Middle Row: A New Zealander civilian : Capt Robertson Commanding Officer of the the Air Station
a War Correspondent : Mrs Robertson : Mr Fraser : Mrs Fraser : Sub Lt Goodwin : Lt White
Mrs Montgomery : Lt Commander Montgomery : Mrs Bassett : Lt Commander Bassett RNZNVR.*

It was time to cross the Atlantic and Peter's duties took them to Ottawa. In meetings with the Senate and House of Commons he reminded Canadian politicians of the principles of the Atlantic Charter (leading people to educational, economic and social democracy). It was a concept dear to his heart, the ideals so closely encapsulating his own vision for the future. Peter and Janet managed a brief visit to see brother Donald in Toronto, then they flew to New York for a private visit with the President and his wife. We are told that the two men had a few hours together. Peter brought the latest news from Winston Churchill and the British War Cabinet, and President Roosevelt discussed the future of Japan's mandated islands which US forces were liberating. Before heading for home, Peter stopped in Washington for talks with officials concerned with establishing a World Bank and an International Monetary Fund.

There was no opportunity for Peter to relax when he got home. He was immersed immediately in the domestic problems that had occupied his ministers during his absence. Groups and individuals had been spreading discontent, and strikes and lockouts had increased a hundredfold. There was a widespread feeling that some were shouldering an unfair burden. Complaints were loud about controls; and the prevention of increases in the price of basic necessities, such as bread and milk and meat, was resented by suppliers. Now that the war clouds were thinning, there was waning support for restrictions, and thoughts of self-indulgence surfaced and stayed.

Labour's carefully controlled economy was under threat. Peter had always hoped that his government could engineer a world where fairness ruled. He and Janet found it frustrating to realise that the socialist creed they had always espoused – a just reward for hard work – was not widely shared. It now seemed there were obstacles in the way and too many people felt it was time to relax and wait for prosperity. The palliative Budget of August 1944 and legislative measures governing paid holiday entitlement, reduced working hours, and the establishment of a minimum wage helped to stabilise the situation and prevented the unravelling of Labour's elaborate economic plans. History shows that the gap between Peter's idealism and the practical realities of day-to-day life in New Zealand would widen in the years ahead.

Several hundred friends and colleagues gathered at Parliament Buildings on 28th August 1944 to mark Peter's milestone birthday. It is recorded that the Prime Minister looked every one of his 60 years – stooped, balding and clearly old before his time. Even on this social occasion, he did not relax. He took the opportunity to urge against self interest and declared his desire for a world that was blind to race. In the past he had rarely discussed racial matters and seemed not to notice the colour of a person's skin; but he was becoming more conscious of the fact that many people were not so tolerant.

Few at that birthday gathering can have realised just how ill the Prime Minister's wife was. Janet had been gradually losing weight and looked gaunt and tired. Her tubercular condition had flared up again, probably exacerbated by shortage of oxygen at times during lengthy plane trips. On her return from a series of meetings of the Maori Women's Health League in the autumn, her doctor ordered her to rest, and in October 1944 she was admitted to hospital. Her anxious husband visited her every day and would read to her, or sometimes he took his government papers with him and worked in her room late at night while she slept. We are told that Peter's vigil was as earnest as hers had been over him for so many years.

Peter was under the weather too. Suffering from another severe staphylococcal infection, he managed to keep going only because doctors dosed him with penicillin. Among the countless issues demanding his attention, Peter centred on the bringing of a shipload of Polish children to New Zealand's shores. It was an issue he was keen to conclude for Janet's sake. In spite of appeals from the country's small Jewish community, the Labour government had not been hospitable to refugees from Europe or immigrants in general – mainly because of a fear they would compete with New Zealanders for jobs.

The youngsters arrived on 1st November, and Peter took a personal interest in developments on Janet's behalf and would tell her of these when he visited the hospital. Initially, it was intended that the children should return to their homeland after the war and they were placed in a refugee camp. As their English improved, some went to stay with Roman Catholic families around New Zealand. Records show that, when Poland was absorbed into the Soviet bloc after the war, Peter decided to allow the young refugees to stay in the country, and he helped many of them to bring close relatives to New Zealand as well. What began as a humanitarian gesture with no strings attached raised the Prime Minister's status in the eyes of many Roman Catholics and many Polish youngsters.

Janet's health was not improving in hospital, but her condition was sufficiently stabilised to enable Peter (as Minister of Island Territories) to visit the Pacific Islands in December 1944. He used the opportunity to familiarise himself with deficiencies in health and education systems by visiting Fiji, Tonga, Samoa and the Cook Islands. He was struck by the primitive conditions and absence of any coherent plan for development. Soon he was thinking about necessary steps to prepare the Pacific Islands for self-government and the establishment of trade links. He kept closely in touch with Janet as his Polynesian tour continued over Christmas and New Year. Diverse official duties ranged from dinner with the Fiji Executive Council to a leper colony hospital visit. As always, Peter made sure he could spend time with New Zealand servicemen in various locations, to share their concerns and listen to their views. Returning home, he prepared to tackle a mountain of work awaiting his attention. The important Yalta conference and the proposed establishment of the United Nations made immediate demands on his working day.

Janet's health began to deteriorate towards the end of January and the decline continued throughout the following month. Peter faced the inevitable: his cherished wife was gravely ill and would not recover. Desperately worried, he conveyed the news to his stepson, Harold, stationed in London. Janet died in hospital on 7th March 1945 with Peter at her side. Her death shocked and saddened the nation, and there was a state funeral service at St John's Presbyterian

Church. Peter was devastated; and granddaughter Alice – feeling she must now look after him – held his hand tightly throughout the service and later as Janet was buried in Karori Cemetery.

There was much to keep Peter busy – major international and domestic issues requiring careful handling. He kept going because he had to. The fact that he could no longer discuss matters with Janet heightened his sense of loss. She and Peter had always worked closely together; and her support, sharp intellect and intuitive wisdom now were gone. He missed her deeply.

His family gathered protectively around him. Rini and ten-year-old Alice went to live with him (Harold joining them when he returned from the war). Living together suited everyone and Rini and Alice helped to fill the void in Peter's life. Rini acted as Peter's official hostess; and Alice became her grandfather's close companion, frequently visiting his office after school, or sitting in the public gallery when he was speaking. Peter was immensely proud of Alice and enjoyed discussing with her plays he had seen and read. He encouraged her growing interest in the theatre and must have been delighted when in later years she won a RADA scholarship.

Events on the world stage in early 1945 heralded the end of conflict with Germany. Allied forces were fighting on Reich territory; and the Red Army occupied Budapest and Warsaw and was heading into East Germany. Hitler's power was crumbling. Only the three warlords (Churchill, Roosevelt and Stalin) attended the Yalta conference but it was an event observed closely by Peter Fraser and all the other Commonwealth Prime Ministers.

Hoping to secure Russian entry into the war against Japan, the US President (clearly unwell) joined Churchill and Stalin in distant Yalta – a venue on which Stalin had insisted. Stalin's duplicity and hidden agenda were yet to be revealed and Roosevelt felt he could trust the Soviet leader. Churchill too accepted him as a man of his word. The conference seems to have been a scene of compromise, of anxiety to avoid confrontation with Stalin, and of political manoeuvring to achieve results. President Roosevelt died two months later, his duel with Stalin unfinished, leaving the Soviet leader to progress unchallenged his secret programme for land-grabbing and the establishment of his totalitarian empire.

Shortly after the Yalta conference, Dresden was bombed and the Allies took Cologne. The Red Army entered Vienna, and German and Italian armies in Italy surrendered after Mussolini's assassination. As the Russians advanced to take Berlin, Adolph Hitler committed suicide. German forces in NW Germany, Holland and Denmark surrendered, and the war in Europe ended on 8th May. The war against Japan continued unabated.

Political historians have recorded the rise of Soviet dominance and the spread of communism. The birth of the United Nations is also recorded, and in this Peter Fraser played a not inconsiderable role in shaping peace for a world emerging at last from the shadow of World War ll. In fact, Peter's role developed appreciably during two months of protracted discussion in San Francisco. He fought doggedly against what he called the excessive authority conferred on the Great Powers, and argued for more rights for small nations. Delegates listened and his views were loudly applauded. In international affairs he acted always on the principle that the guiding motives should be those of morality rather than expediency. That explained his unyielding opposition to the veto rights of the Great Powers on the UN Security Council. His efforts were unsuccessful but it was an honourable defeat. The World Security Charter to establish the United Nations (the organisation of over 150 countries set up to promote international peace, security and co-operation) was finally signed on 26th June 1945.

A Founding Father of the United Nations
San Francisco 1945

In a letter to Peter dated 23rd June 1945 E.R. Stettinius, the US Secretary of State wrote:

'Before we leave San Francisco, I wish to thank you personally for the outstanding part you have played in the drafting of the Charter. No one at the conference has brought higher ideals to our work nor more persistence in seeking to give effect to them. The Chapter on Trusteeship, which owes so much to your guidance, will, I am confident, prove to be one of the most historic of our achievements. You have contributed much to making it a sure basis for the advancement and welfare of untold millions. I sincerely trust that the many improvements in the Charter for which your efforts had been responsible will prove a source of enduring satisfaction to you. It has been an honour and a privilege to be associated with you in this work.'

Peter returned home to wide acclaim for his outstanding statesmanship but, characteristically, he tried to avoid the personal publicity. As he saw it, he had simply done his best. Others regarded him as a founding father of the United Nations and San Francisco as the pinnacle of his career. In the 1946 New Year Honours list Peter's name led all the rest, when he was made a Companion of Honour by His Majesty the King in recognition of his conspicuous service of national importance. He was the first New Zealander to be so honoured.

The conflict in Europe had ended while Peter was away, but one million men were still at war against Japan. American atomic bombs destroyed Hiroshima and Nagasaki, and Japan surrendered unconditionally on 15th July 1945. Six years of war were over. It is estimated that World War ll produced 57 million casualties; and the atrocities that had been exposed – and those yet to be revealed – showed that mankind was capable of sinking to new depths of inhumanity. However, just then the world was enjoying its first days of peace after so many bitter, war-torn years. For many prisoners-of-war freed from appalling conditions in Japanese camps, VJ Day was the first day of the rest of their lives. Death had been a close companion.

Dominion Leaders sign agreement at 10 Downing Street, London.
L to R: Gen Smuts : Mackenzie King : Winston Churchill : John Curtin : Peter Fraser
16 May 1944

CHAPTER 7

1946 – 1950

The enormous task of reconverting New Zealand's economy to a peace-time basis would occupy Peter and his ministers for the next three years. The needs of servicemen returning home had to be met, while avoiding the extremes of gross inflation or exaggerated unemployment. During this same period Peter continued his world-wide travels. He was not always well but visited London several times for conferences and worked in close harmony with Prime Minister Clement Attlee. The post-war swing towards change had brought Winston Churchill's surprise defeat in Britain's 1945 general election. While in London in January 1946 for the first General Assembly of the United Nations, Peter was invited to Buckingham Palace, where King George VI invested him with the Companion of Honour insignia.

Peter Fraser was the only Dominion Leader to remain in power after the post war elections

Respiratory problems kept Peter away from his office in July and August 1948 but when he returned he prepared for another round of overseas meetings. These took him to London for a meeting of the Commonwealth leaders at Downing Street and to Paris for the UN General Assembly. He took the opportunity to fly to Germany. He visited five cities, including a divided Berlin, and became increasingly alarmed by Russian tactics. Trouble was looming on so many fronts and the unanimity of nations expressed at San Francisco was not being achieved.

Peter's schedule saw him back in Paris at the UN in November. He had talked at one stage of being home by Christmas, but he needed time to think – well away from domestic concerns, including the forthcoming general election.

He spent three days in Ireland. He dined with the Irish President, Sean Kelly, and the Indian High Commissioner, Krishna Menon. Before returning to London he received an honorary LLD degree of the University of Ireland in Dublin. Dining at Buckingham Palace immediately after Christmas, he was the first of the Commonwealth ministers to see the royal baby, Prince Charles. Then he left London by car.

Peter enjoys a cup of tea at Rhynie House, Fearn 1948.
Ian Ross and his sisters Miss Nan Ross and Miss Grace Ross

As always when he wanted time to think, Peter yearned for the Scottish Highlands. He stopped in Edinburgh, visited the Tummel-Garry hydro scheme, broadcast a New Year message to New Zealand, and arrived in Inverness on 30th December. It was bitterly cold and there were blizzards but he enjoyed a warm reception and a splendid civic dinner staged in Tain on New Year's Eve when he joined in honouring two former provosts of the burgh, Mr W. J. Munro and Mr W. Fraser who, between them, had served 60 years on the Council. Portraits in oil were presented by Provost David Geekie's wife to the ex-provosts. In his reply to Bailie Fletcher's toast to 'New Zealand' Peter said that Ross-shire men had made their mark in many parts of the world and that the present satisfactory situation in New Zealand was due, to a large extent, to four men of the county who had, all in their different fields, made great contributions to the development of the Dominion. They were all Mackenzies – Sir John Mackenzie of Ardross, who had been Minister for Lands in New Zealand; Mr Roderick Mackenzie of Plockton, who was at one time Minister of Works; Sir Thomas Mackenzie, a native of Invergordon, who was Prime Minister for a short period; and Mr Scobie Mackenzie, a native of Tain, who was a prominent politician.

He had his first Hogmanay in Hill of Fearn since emigrating some 40 years earlier, and he spent several happy days with friends and cousins around his boyhood home and at Portmahomack. In Inverness with Tom Skinner he telephoned many friends. The short holiday was a tonic for Peter, but neither he nor his friends realised it was the last time they would be together.

Peter welcomes in the New Year of 1949 at Rhynie House, Fearn
L to R: K M Sleight (Private Secretary) : Miss Nan Ross : Miss Grace Ross: Tom Skinner
Peter Fraser : Miss M Weybonny (Assistant Secretary)

Peter had plunged into his work with renewed vigour after Janet's passing and would not spare himself. In January 1949 he flew to Canada for a meeting with Prime Minister Saint Laurent. Later he discussed old times with Mackenzie King and, seeking new markets for New Zealand butter, held trade talks with government ministers in Ottawa. He visited Donald in Toronto and had a short meeting with US President Harry Truman in Washington. He returned home on 26th January 1949 to find a backlog of business awaiting his attention, including pressing Maori affairs. Concerned observers commented on his pallor.

Still immersed in thought about the changing world and having realised earlier than others that dealing with the Soviet Union was a one-way street, Peter turned his attention again to defence. Communist troops were in China and too close for comfort. In one of his finest speeches, Peter pleaded with the 600 delegates at the Labour Party's annual conference to give authority for compulsory military service within strictly defined limits. A national referendum produced a three-to-one majority in support of conscription in New Zealand. Many who opposed the plan came from Labour ranks.

Peter celebrated his 65th birthday on 28th August 1949, and on 3rd October he celebrated 31 years in Parliament. He was 'Father of the House', having been an MP longer than any other current member. He modestly brushed aside speculation that he might move to the House of Lords as Lord Fraser of Fearn. With the election only weeks away, Peter had no immediate plans to retire.

The Labour Party had won the 1946 election by a narrow margin and problems beset it continually thereafter. As the 1949 election appeared on the horizon, the biggest threat to government came from the industrial unions and there were strikes and ugly scenes. Peter stood firm on the policy of wage control. An increasing number of New Zealanders felt that his government was losing touch with them. They were tired of regulations, and it is recorded that many now expected from the state as of right what they had once dreamed about or accepted gratefully. Materialism had replaced socialism. Peter was conscious too of the generation gap in his own ministerial team. New younger members worried him: they were intellectually confident, less respectful of authority and ready to kick over the traces.

Peter Fraser presides over his retiring Labour Cabinet of late 1949

The prospect that Labour would win another term in office was bleak. Public indifference and hostility from the press were clear indications that the country wanted a change – and that was indeed the case. Everywhere Peter went he encountered apathy. The swing against Labour was evident. Nevertheless, when the axe fell it shocked many.

Peter graciously conceded defeat and held his last Cabinet meeting on 5th December 1949. He vacated the Prime Minister's residence and accepted an invitation from Harold and Rini to share their new home. His vast collection of books and papers were shifted to the Library Wing in Parliamentary Buildings. Lots of personal correspondence and farewell functions filled the December days; then Peter was confined to bed for several weeks over Christmas and New Year with a painful blood clot in his leg. Harold cared for him assiduously.

The Labour Party was a victim of the very prosperity it had developed; but Peter took his place on the opposition benches in the New Year. It grieved him greatly to watch the new National government making radical changes to the country's economic structure. Some Labour members took solace in the belief that the National Party would falter quickly, opening the way for their early return to office. This pre-supposed that Labour opposition was still a formidable force. It was not. As the weeks passed, it became clear that Peter lacked the physical strength to maintain an effective onslaught against the new Prime Minister. He was in no fit state to lead a fightback. Though only 65, Peter was worn out. Constant pressures over many years, poor diet, little rest and no exercise had taken their toll, and the dangerous blood clot lingered in his leg.

It was not in his nature to quit, but Peter did find that being in opposition had compensations. He had time to relax. He had been influential in the establishment of the country's National Orchestra and managed to attend a spring concert in Auckland and two in Wellington in July. He was present at the public meeting to launch the Alex Lindsay String Orchestra at the end of May 1950 and keenly awaited the arrival of Sadler's Wells Ballet company and Margot Fonteyn. He had always tried to make time to see good theatrical productions (especially Shakespeare) and had maintained regular contact with Dame Sybil Thorndike and her husband, Lewis Casson, over many years. He had also enjoyed meeting Sir Laurence Olivier and Vivien Leigh, when the Old Vic Company visited New Zealand. Now he was able to encourage Alice's growing theatrical talent; and together they saw actor Robert Morley at the Opera House, 'Twelfth Night' performed by the Wellington Thespians and the musical 'Oklahoma'.

Alice and her mother sailed for London in August 1950. She was to take up a drama scholarship and Rini was visiting doctors. Harold joined his wife a few weeks later, and Rini's brother Tim Armstrong, moved in to keep Peter company.

Alice remembered her grandfather standing at the end of the wharf – a lonely figure – waving as the ship departed. Her letters to him were full of detail about her drama training and her new surroundings. Peter read them avidly and dipped into biographies and cowboy stories during quiet evenings.

Shortly before Parliament assembled in October, Peter had a stroke affecting his left arm and leg. In hospital, congestion of the lungs and pleurisy were followed by a heart attack. Peter had no physical reserves and nearly died when pneumonia set in, but his condition stabilised with careful nursing. Two further heart attacks confirmed the seriousness of his condition, and it was realised that he was unlikely to return to Parliament if he recovered.

Goodwill messages flooded in, and the King and Queen cabled their best wishes. Friends and family gathered round, and Harold flew home from London with welcome news of Rini and Alice. Peter rallied; and in early December he was well enough to read newspapers, and to concern himself with the war in Korea and the welfare of much-loved staff members, who had been an essential part of his life and work in politics. After ten weeks, Peter was allowed out of bed for a while. He sat in a chair and read. Next day (Tuesday 12th December) he suffered a fourth heart attack and gradually slipped into unconsciousness. A pulmonary embolism snuffed out the life of a truly remarkable man.

Hundreds upon hundreds of tributes poured in. They came from personal friends throughout the Commonwealth, Europe and the United States; from Clement Attlee and other renowned statesmen and from worldwide governments Messages of sympathy and condolence came from foreign diplomats, industrial leaders, trade unionists, Labour Party members and individuals who had known and worked with Peter during his long years of service. A very touching message was received from King George.

His body lay in state in Parliament Buildings, and members came from all sections of the community to pay their respects to a loved and trusted friend. Representatives of the Jewish community remembered how Peter had identified himself with the Zionist Movement and his assistance in the creation of the new State of Israel. His charitable outlook had led to New Zealand opening its doors to give sanctuary to hundreds of the war's child victims, and Poles spoke of his support as a great benefactor. Wellington's large Chinese community recalled his attendance as an honoured guest at their public and private celebrations, and his presentation in 1948 with the decoration of the Special Grand Cordon of the Order of the Brilliant Star (by direction of the Chinese government). The Chinese people had deep regard for Peter's work and desired particularly to associate the name of Janet Fraser with their tribute, for she too had done outstanding work in helping the cause of starving children in China.

For many years, Maori had regarded Peter as one of their leaders. He had won their hearts by his interest in their welfare. Painfully aware that they had lost a true and loyal friend, they held a moving tribute before the funeral. Some 200 men and women assembled round the catafalque, and many wept throughout the ceremony and orations. Peter had hoped to study the early history of Maori in his retirement years, and now there was palpable grief for the departure of their beloved 'White Heron'.

Peter had been a natural leader evoking complete loyalty and faithful service from all who worked for him. Only those close to him knew of the endless good he preferred to do quietly and privately; and it would be remembered always how he and Janet almost denuded their home of life's necessities to help others in Wellington during the Depression years. Friends spoke in glowing terms of his sincerity, his kindness, his warmhearted friendliness, his humility and companionship. They knew that, though forthright in expressing his opinions, he had never consciously done anything that would leave a feeling of rancour; and they recalled his tireless work for the old, for the young, and for the rights and privileges of women.

The funeral service conducted by Peter's friend, the Rev. W. J. Pellow, was one of simple and impressive dignity. Huge crowds lined the streets between Parliament Buildings and St John's Presbyterian Church, and along the route to the cemetery overlooking the city that had grown to love and honour him. He was buried alongside his beloved Janet on the the beautiful slopes of Karori, a resting place echoing the beauty of the Scottish Highlands.

N.Z. HERALD, 13.12.50

CHAPTER 8

EPILOGUE

Memorial services took place in Fearn Abbey and in Tain during the weeks that followed Peter Fraser's death. His Highland friends were deeply affected, for they had enjoyed his company so recently. They recalled the happy atmosphere during his last holiday among them. They remembered his delight when the Fearn Abbey bell rang out at midnight across the fields to Rhynie during their special Hogmanay celebrations; then, Peter had shared the warm feelings it aroused and his sense of real belonging.

Happy memories have been long cherished; but the years pass quickly, a new generation grows up and collective memory fades. Yet Peter has not been forgotten in Fearn. It had seemingly been his wish to set up a prize for class excellence at the school where he had received his education, but he died before being able to implement such a gift. A memorial committee to raise funds was formed by his old schoolfriends – Captain George Gordon of Elmbank, Kenneth MacLeod (resident in Tain) and George M.Smith (a jeweller in Dingwall) – under the

Unveiling of the Memorial Plaque in memory of Peter Fraser, Hill of Fearn School. 1956
L to R: Thomas Skinner : Angus MacLeod, Headmaster : Mrs Margaret Palmer
Mr Ian Ross - Convener of the Memorial Committee

convenorship of Ian Ross of Rhynie and with Fearn schoolmaster, Angus MacLeod, acting as secretary and treasurer. A simple ceremony took place in Hill of Fearn School on 12th December 1956. Former classmate, Mrs Margaret Palmer, travelled from Lanark to unveil a plaque in the headmaster's classroom in memory of the school's most distinguished former pupil; and a message was read from the High Commissioner of New Zealand, Mr Clifton Webb, paying warm tribute to the late Peter Fraser. The prize fund was established, and a modest memorial tablet was commissioned for the outside gable of Fraser Cottage.

Over the years, people have travelled from the world's four corners to visit Peter's childhood home. Mrs Dinah Gray made everyone who called most welcome and insisted that all should visit the little cobbler's shop – the Hill of Fearn 'House of Commons', where Peter had received his political initiation. Members of the New Zealand government and others were grateful for her devotion to keeping alive the memory of Peter Fraser; and, on special occasions, a limousine would whisk her away from Fraser Cottage for afternoon tea at the Royal Hotel in Tain with New Zealand ministers, High Commissioners, officials, historians and film production company members.

Peter's beloved grand-daughter visited Hill of Fearn school in 1972 and called again at Fraser Cottage in 1989, leaving a friendly personal message in Mrs Gray's visitors' book. After her dramatic arts studies in London, Alice Fraser had become a renowned actress in both New Zealand and the United Kingdom. She had a particular affection for the Pitlochry Theatre in Perthshire. Her last visit there was in September 2004 for, sadly, Alice died a few months later at her home in Wellington, New Zealand.

The New Zealand historian and author, Dr Michael King, wrote to Mrs Gray in March 1984 to enquire if anything would be happening in August of that year to celebrate the 100th anniversary of Peter's birth. The New Zealand High Commissioner, Mr William Young, travelled north from London with his wife to take part in a ceremony at the school, and Mrs Gray at Fraser Cottage received a framed inscription – a message from Sir Robert Muldoon, the Leader of the NZ National Party.

More recently, on 30th May 2003, the newly refurbished library at Hill of Fearn School was dedicated to its most illustrious former pupil. Senior pupils David Robb and Leanne Ross outlined the importance of Peter's life as Prime Minister of New Zealand; then Jean Cheyne declared the Peter Fraser Library open. Former school secretary, Mrs Cheyne, had also organised an exhibition at the school on Peter's life and work.

Mr Stanley Munro, headteacher, welcomes Mr William Young, High Commissioner for New Zealand on his visit to Fearn School to celebrate the Centenary of Peter Fraser's birth.

28 August 1984

In the following year a request was received from Peter Leslie and Ereti Mitchell of the New Zealand Society (Scotland) for permission to visit Hill of Fearn School. A delightful afternoon in June 2004 introduced the children to New Zealand culture and Maori traditions. Before classes finished for the day, the pupils performed a short programme of Maori dance and song, culminating in a rendering of the famous haka rugby chant by the boys. An unexpected honour was bestowed on the school when a framed letter was presented from Helen Clark, to-day's Prime Minister of New Zealand. She closed her letter by saying: *'His contribution to making New Zealand a better place was immense. We thank Fearn School for the role it played in Peter Fraser's life.'*

His was a life that made the world a better place for countless thousands.

ROYAL BURGH OF TAIN.

RECEPTION

In The Royal Hotel, Tain
On Monday, 4th August, 1941

To

THE RIGHT HON. PETER FRASER
PRIME MINISTER OF
THE DOMINION OF NEW ZEALAND

Admit *K. M. Macleod, Esq. and Mrs. Macleod*   A. W.

P.T.O.

ROYAL BURGH OF TAIN.

RECEPTION

In The Royal Hotel, Tain
On Monday, 4th August, 1941

To

THE RIGHT HON. PETER FRASER
PRIME MINISTER OF
THE DOMINION OF NEW ZEALAND

Admit *Miss Margaret Macleod*

A. W. GRAY,
Town Clerk.

ROYAL BURGH OF TAIN.

The Provost, Magistrates and Councillors of the Royal Burgh of Tain
request the honour of the company of

Miss Margaret Macleod

on the occasion of the

PRESENTATION OF THE FREEDOM OF THE BURGH TO

The Right Hon. PETER FRASER
PRIME MINISTER OF THE DOMINION OF NEW ZEALAND
In Queen Street Church, Tain, on Monday, 4th August, 1941
At 12 o'clock Noon.

A.

R.S.V.P.

ROYAL BURGH OF TAIN.

PRESENTATION OF THE FREEDOM OF THE BURGH

To

THE RIGHT HON. PETER FRASER
PRIME MINISTER OF NEW ZEALAND.

PROVOST'S PRIVATE LUNCHEON.

Provost William Fraser has the honour to request the Company of

K. M. MACLEOD, ESQ.

to a Private Luncheon to be held in the Royal Hotel, Tain
on Monday, 4th August, 1941, at 3 o'clock p.m.

COUNCIL CHAMBERS,
TAIN, July, 1941.

R.S.V.P.

PHOTOGRAPHS COURTESY OF:

The Imperial War Museum, London.

| P 39 | H1250 (Upper) | P 41 | HU87557 | P 48 A24607 |
| P 49 | A24605 | P 53 | NYT 80405 | P 54 HU55580 |

The Alexander Turnbull Library and National Archives, Wellington, New Zealand

P 17	National Archives	P 19	029818	P 20 PAColl-6304-51
P 21	018612	P 23	055145	P 24 005062
P 26	C4745	P 34	DA-01097	P 35 DA-01096
P 43		P 47	DA-05811	P 47 DA-05818
P 58	F-30130			

P 61   B-056-003 - Copyright: New Zealand Herald - Gordon Minhinnick Sketch

ITN Archives - British Pathe   P 9 and P 40

Tain Museum   P 10

The John Curtin Prime Ministerial Library, Perth, Australia

| P 46 | JCPML00018/28 – | Records of Frederick McLaughlin |
| P 55 | JCPML00376/77 | |

The People's Journal   P 56

Aberdeen Press and Journal   P 39   (Lower) and P 62

The North Star   P 64

Map   P 32   Copyright: Wendy Price